Bedtime Stories

A Child's Collection of Poems

GORDON BOSTIC

Primix Publishing
East Brunswick Office Evolution
1 Tower Center Boulevard, Ste 1510
East Brunswick, NJ 08816
www.primixpublishing.com
Phone: 1-800-538-5788

Published by Primix Publishing: 12/09/2024

ISBN: 979-8-88703-408-9(sc)
ISBN: 979-8-88703-409-6(e)

Library of Congress Control Number: 2024917429

Any people depicted in stock imagery provided by iStock are models, and such images are being used for illustrative purposes only.

Certain stock imagery © iStock.

Because of the dynamic nature of the Internet, any web addresses or links contained in this book may have changed since publication and may no longer be valid. The views expressed in this work are solely those of the author and do not necessarily reflect the views of the publisher, and the publisher hereby disclaims any responsibility for them.

To my sister and my wife who provided the support; and my daughter and grandson, who provided the inspiration.

The Little Comet

The little comet wished to be
A star that shined at night.
So it could stay in one place and
Not always be in flight.

His mother said, "You need to learn
To enjoy what you are.
You are a little comet, dear,
And not a little star."

He was not happy, but he'd learn
To be the best he could.
He was a comet on patrol
As ev'ry comet should.

A Walk Along the Beach

I like to walk along the beach
To see what I can see.
To find treasures I can take home
That mean something to me.

Like seashells that have washed ashore,
Or driftwood that came home.
Or seaweed that has draped the shore
That now looks so alone.

I keep my treasures in a box,
I keep in easy reach.
So I remember what it's like
To walk along the beach.

Who's in the Mirror?

I look into the mirror
And wonder what I'll see.
Could it be a crocodile
That's looking back at me?

Or could it be a hedgehog
That my reflection shows?
Or perhaps an anteater,
Who has a funny nose.

I look into the mirror
And wonder what I'll see,
When I find who's looking back
Is no one else but me!

The Red Balloon

Once I had a red balloon.
I loved to watch it fly.
How it bounced within the breeze
As it would touch the sky.

It would hop upon the wind
As it would pull and sway.
As if fighting to be free
Or simply get away.

I clung on to my balloon
For what it meant to me.
Then I had a change of heart
And set my balloon free.

The Honey Bee

Bernie is a honey bee
Who used to guard the hive.
Now he is a worker bee
And gets to go outside.

He will flit from bloom to bloom
For that is what he does.
So they can make the honey
That sets the hive abuzz.

For some pollen he will search
Down in the meadow green.
Where he'll collect all he can
To bring back to the queen.

All the Fishes

See the fishes in the pond
And how they swim near and yond.
Maybe some have special bonds.
All the fishes in the pond.

See the fishes in the lake.
Some are little. Some are great.
Some may even leave a wake.
All the fishes in the lake.

See the fishes in the sea.
Some are large and some are wee.
Some may be as big as me.
All the fishes in the sea.

The Seashell

I came upon a seashell
That wished to speak to me.
When I put it to my ear
It sounded like the sea.

How wonderful, I had thought,
That I could hear the sea.
Even when its far away,
It still can speak to me.

When I'm sad I cannot go
And walk beside the sea.
At least I have my seashell
Which always speaks to me.

Lay Me Down

Lay me down. Now to sleep.

For my soul is God's to keep.

Little star, way up high,

Keep me with your watchful eye.

Let me rest. Let me dream.

'Til the morning light is seen.

Then I'll wake. Now restored.

Refreshed to live, one day more

Not Ready for Bed

I'm not ready for my bed,
Though my eyes are weary red.
I can barely lift my head.
I'm not ready for my bed.

I have way too much to do.
While the sky is still so blue,
My day can't be almost through.
I have way too much to do.

I'm not ready for my bed,
Though my eyelids feel like lead
And I have a sleepy head.
I'm not ready for my bed.

One by One

See the ants march one by one
In their search for tiny crumbs.
Far beneath the midday sun,
In a line of one by one.

See the ants march one by one
On a quest they have begun.
They will work till they are done
As they march past one by one.

See the ants march one by one
As they gather tiny crumbs.
Bringing food for ev'ryone.
Then their work is truly done.

As the Trains Go By

I like to watch the trains go by
As they wind down the tracks,
And listen to the rhythmic sounds
Of their clickity-clacks.

I have a spot above the tracks
From which I like to spy,
And count the cars that make the train
As it goes roaring by.

I see boxcars and the caboose.
I see some coal cars too,
And flat cars with their trailers in
Colors of red and blue.

Too soon the train has come and gone
And left me far behind.
But I can always see the train
From pictures in my mind.

The Bare Hare

All the bunnies in the dell
Were so proud of their hair.
They thought of holding contests
To see who was best hare.

Then there came a bunny who
Had very little hair.
All the bunnies laughed at him
And said that he was bare.

They taunted him with their chants
And called him "the bare hare."
But he would just ignore them,
Pretending not to care.

Then as he began to grow,
His fur had grown as well.
'Til he was the envy of
The bunnies in the dell.

The Little Star

Once there was a little star
Whose light refused to shine.
He had tried his hardest, but
It failed, time after time.

He had thought to ask the sun
For help of any kind,
But the sun was unable
To get his light to shine.

Then he had approached the moon,
To help his light to shine.
Who told him, think happy thoughts,
And it will come with time.

So the little star relaxed,
And thought of happy times.
Then found that his light returned
And he more brightly shined.

The Bird Bath

My father built a bird bath
And placed it by a tree.
From my window I would watch
The splashing chickadee.

Then the robins would swoop in
And they would drink their fill.
Followed by the blue jays and
A noisy whip-o-will.

Next would come the cardinals,
As red as I have seen,
And sit upon the edges
Where they would primp and preen.

Then the birds would all be gone,
As it would stand alone,
Waiting for the coming day
When all the birds come home.

19

There Go the Ducklings

There go the ducklings, two by two,
As if they're on parade.
While marching to the river's edge
Where they can swim and bathe.

There go the ducklings in a rush
To go off and explore,
To see what's in the river's bed
And what's along the shore.

There go the ducklings in a row
Their mother in the lead,
So that she can look out for them
And help if there's a need.

The Sunset

I love to watch the sunset,
So peaceful and serene.
With all its many colors
As if a painted scene.

Then the twilight follows next,
As colors start to age,
And the stars begin to shine
Upon the twilight stage.

'Til the sky's completely dark
And daylight's gone to rest.
As I watch the twinkling stars,
I know that I'll be next.

The Lazy Grasshopper

Once there was a grasshopper
Who had refused to try.
He was lazy to a fault
Just trying to get by.

He laughed at those who would work,
As if they were a fool,
And lounged about, lazily,
Down by the swimming pool.

So when wintertime arrived
And all the snow had come.
All the rest had been well fed,
But he'd only a crumb.

23

All Who Learned to Share

The red ants and the black ants
Did not see eye to eye.
The black ants wanted the crumbs
The red ants were to spy.

Battle lines were quickly drawn,
With each ready for war.
The crumbs had lain in between
As something to fight for.

Then one ant, who's very brave,
Suggested that they share,
So the peace had been restored
To all who learned to share.

The Fireworks

We'd always watch the fireworks
Ev'ry Fourth of July
And marvel at the colors
As they lit up the sky.

The colorful explosions
That drew gasps from the throng.
That served to paint the heavens,
I could watch all night long.

Though, sometimes they hurt my ears,
They're wonderful to see.
Fireworks that command the night
That burn so prettily.

I Love the Feel of Christmas

I love the feel of Christmas;
The tinsel and the lights.
The smell of Christmas cookies,
Which are purely delights.

The sounds of Christmas music
Which blare everywhere.
The sparkle of Christmas trees
And crispness of the air.

The wonder of store displays.
The snow, should it decide,
Ol' Saint Nick, eight reindeer,
Packages and sleigh ride.

I love the feel of Christmas
And what it means to me.
The birth of baby Jesus,
And what he came to be.

My Cat

My cat believes she is the queen.
My house is where she rules.
She spends her days lazing about
As if there were no rules.

She's constantly on a sojourn
From windowsill to bed.
Where in between she takes her time
Sleeping with buried head.

She believes that I'm her servant
Who's there to serve her needs.
And if she finds her dish empty,
The one to whom she pleads.

But after dark, when we're alone,
My lap is what she finds.
I pet her while she purrs content,
Sharing the tie that binds.

The Lonely Little Seashell

The little seashell was lonely
As it had washed ashore.
For there weren't as many seashells
As on the ocean's floor.

He felt the waves wash over him,
Pushing him towards shore.
The poor lonely little seashell,
Swept from the ocean's floor.

He wondered if other seashells
Were waiting on the shore,
And if they'd gladly welcome him
When he had washed ashore.

But then he felt the tide had turned,
And pulled him from the shore.
Where, hopefully, he'd return to
Live on the ocean's floor.

Halloween

Its nearly time for Halloween
When trick-or-treaters run.
It is the one night in the year
When scary things are fun.

When we light our jack-o-lanterns
And turn the lights down low,
Then set out to go house to house
Of people that we know.

So when our goodie bags are full
Of treats given away,
We can watch a scary movie
To end a perfect day.

The Circus

I love it when the circus comes.
There's magic in the air.
For it is full of wonderment
Not seen just anywhere.

Like elephants who're on parade
Around the center ring.
As trapeze artists touch the sky
High above ev'rything.

There are also acrobats and
The man who walks the wire.
And the man who has trained the cats
To leap through hoops of fire.

Then as the show comes to an end,
And all pause to exhale,
The applause becomes thunderous
As we dare to inhale.

The Starfish

I found a tiny starfish
That washed up on the shore
As I walked along the beach
When going to the store.

It looked like a sheriff's badge
From stories I have read
Or a star that fell to earth
From the sky overhead.

It was pretty, in its way,
Abandoned on the shore.
The starfish that I'd found
When going to the store.

The Meadow

I like to run in the meadow
When it's a sunny day.
And stop and watch the animals
As I am on my way.

I watch to see the bunnies run
From unseen enemy.
I watch the groundhogs sun themselves
Or waddle lazily.

The butterflies have multiplied
Since last time I was here.
And if I should look close enough,
I just can see the deer.

The meadow is a happy place
Where I can spend my day.
Just watching all the animals
As I am on my way.

Tippy

Tippy was a lonely pup
Who did not have a home.
But he had a lot of friends
Who'd gladly share their home.

The rabbit said he could stay
Inside his rabbit hole,
But Tippy was a puppy
And not much of a mole.

Frog offered his lily pad
But that would never do.
Tippy was too big for it
And surely would fall through.

Then Tippy happened upon
A little boy to tend,
Who wanted to take him home
And become his best friend.

So Tippy had found a home
Where he could run and play,
And a boy who loved him so

For all of Tippy's days.

The Circus Superstar

Once there was a flea named Pete
Who was a circus star.
He would always wow the crowd
When he would lift the bar.

He would do his high-wire act,
Then swing on the trapeze.
Next he tamed the tiger ants
Before he rode the bees.

They would always feature Pete
As he's a one-man show.
He's the circus superstar
Wherever they would go.

The Storm Cloud

Brianna was a storm cloud
But did not want to be.
She wished to be fluffy white
And bright for all to see.

She felt gloomy all the time
And heavy with the rain.
To her mother she had turned
To whimper and complain.

Her mother said that storm clouds
Offer much more than show.
When they come, they bring the rain,
And that makes all things grow.

Then Brianna took great pride
In helping all things live.
She knew she had a purpose
And gifts she had to give.

The Fallen Star

Once there was a fallen star
Who wished to return home.
Earth was such a tiny place
He had no room to roam.

But once a star has fallen,
It never can return.
He must look for other ways
So his light could still burn.

He had found it curious
That he was all alone.
Where were other fallen stars,
Some whom he may have known?

Then it had occurred to him
Where other stars had gone.
So he became a firefly
Whose light would still burn on.

You Have Only Two

The centipede has many legs
But you have only two.
It cannot run quite as fast
But it tries to make do.

The spider has multiple eyes,
But you have only two.
It only sees in black and white
While you see colors too.

The millipede has many arms
But you have only two.
It can wave to many friends,
But cannot hug like you.

My Teddy Bear

My teddy bear is my best friend.
I take him ev'rywhere.
He knows my secrets and my faults
But really does not care.

Whenever I am feeling sad
I know he's close at hand.
And he listens to my stories
But he'll make no demand.

I can never feel too lonely
As long as he's in town.
My teddy bear is my best friend,
Who is so soft and brown.

The Model Train

I had a friend who had a train
He set up once a year.
He pulled it out at Christmastime
To help build Christmas cheer.

It had an old locomotive
That pulled five railroad cars.
And it had a bright red caboose
That always trailed the cars.

Whenever he would set it up,
The hours we would spend,
Watching the train circle the track
And run from end to end.

The Pond

When I hike, I like to walk
Down by the little pond.
It's become a special place
Of which I'm very fond.

Where frogs sit on lily pads
Above where tadpoles play.
Where catfish skim the bottom
And swim around all day.

Dragonflies will sweep the pond
To snack on mosquitoes.
Where I can remove my shoes
And lightly dip my toes.

Mud Puddles

I like to look for mud puddles.
The biggest I can see.
So I can run and jump in them
And have them splash on me.

I like to wade through mud puddles
And feel the water part,
As if it were a special ride
In an amusement park.

I like to run through mud puddles
And hope they're long and deep.
So I can feel the silt and mud
Go squish beneath my feet.

Bath Time

I cannot wait for bath time
When I can grab my boats
And launch them upon the sea
As my flotilla floats.

I can make my boats go fast
By pushing with my hands.
I can sink them, if I wish,
With water I command.

I can splash to make the waves
My boats will have to ride.
And when my bath's almost done,
I set them out to dry.

Rex, the Talking Squirrel

He was sitting on a fence post,
And seemed all in a whirl.
Then paused to introduce himself
As Rex, the talking squirrel.

He was gray with a bushy tail
And had great big brown eyes.
He was wiser than he appeared
And what his form belies.

I found Rex to be talkative
With lots of things to say,
So now we spend our evenings
Talking the night away.

Haley Was a Shooting Star

Haley was a shooting star
That roamed the galaxy.
Each day's a new adventure
With brand-new things to see.

She'd been to all the planets,
And seen Pluto, of course.
She had flown through Saturn's rings,
Though, twice she did change course.

She had raced a meteor
(A race she all but won)
And dared to be burned alive
When circling the sun.

Each day's a new adventure
For one busy as she.
Haley was a shooting star
That roamed the galaxy.

Creatures of the Sea

When I think of all the creatures
That live under the sea,
I find it unbelievable
It can hold that many.

Like sharks and whales and porpoises
All live within the sea.
As do the swordfish and the fluke
And sea anemone.

Like dolphins and electric eels
And the gentle sea horse;
Like sea urchin and mackerel
And the minnows, of course.

The thought of it amazes me,
To know the sea can hide
So many different creatures
That live beneath the tide.

Our Day at the Fair

When I was young, the day we prized,
Was going to the fair.
With all the things to see and do
And ev'ryone was there.

We would stroll through the livestock barns,
To see cows, pigs, and sheep.
Then we'd visit all the displays
To see the crops they'd reap.

Then all the treats that we'd devour,
From donuts to ice cream;
The candy apples and popcorn
As good as I could dream.

We'd follow a tight schedule
To take in the best show.
And, maybe, visit the grandstand
For headliners we know.

But before the day was complete,
We'd wander the midway
Riding on all the rides we could,
Then calling it a day.

Rainy Days

What can we do on rainy days
When we can't go outside;
When the weather becomes so bleak
We have to stay inside?

We could color inside the lines
Or, maybe, read a book.
We could construct a Lego fort
Or, maybe, take a look

To see if mother needs some help
With any household chore.
Or we could simply make believe
Our room's become a store.

There's lots to do on rainy days
When we can't go outside.
We can use imagination
To try things we've not tried.

Herman, the Crabby Crab

Herman was a crabby crab
Who complained all the time.
He was never satisfied
Despite response or clime.

'Til one day he met a gull
Much crabbier than he.
Who'd go on with his complaints,
Driving Herman crazy.

Once the gull had gone its way,
He made a solemn vow.
That he'd not again complain
And that would start right now.

Herman was a happy crab
Who never would complain.
He was always satisfied
Come sunshine or the rain.

The Game They Loved

Soccer has been my parents' game,
So I want to play too.
To know the ins and outs of it
Just as my parents do.

I want to be part of a team
Just like my parents' team;
And have the skills my parents have,
As hard as that may seem.

I want to play on the same field
On which my parents played,
And enjoy the game they have loved
For the length that they've played.

Sailing on the Stream

Sometimes on warm summer days
We'd go down to the stream.
We would take our boats with us
To act out what we dream.

Some of us would go upstream
Where we could launch each boat.
While some of us stayed downstream
To catch them as they'd float.

We'd take turns which way we went
Either upstream or down,
And we'd take turns launching boats
Or catching them when found.

We would spend most of the day
Just letting our boats sail.
Basking in a summer's day
That we'll remember well.

The Bunnies in My Yard

I love to watch the bunnies
That live somewhere in my yard
And how they will hop and play
While they're always on their guard.

Sometimes they will startle me
When they're busy with their play.
They will catch me unaware
Then they'll turn and run away.

I watch their little noses twitch
As they watch me with regard,
The bunnies who eat my grass
And live somewhere in my yard.

Your Birthday

Tomorrow is your birthday when
We celebrate your birth,
And all the joy that you have brought
Since coming to this earth.

There'll be balloons and pony rides
And lots and lots of fun.
There'll be a special birthday cake
And ice cream when we're done.

And when the party's almost done,
Your gifts you will explore.
When you open the packages
Your guests left by the door.

Then when the party is complete
And all have gone to bed;
Your dreams are dreams about the day
When so much joy was spread.

My Bedtime Stories

I love my bedtime stories
To finish off my day.
I love the pace of the words
As much as what they say.

I love the new adventures
Presented ev'ry night.
Amazed at the characters
And what may be their plight.

They all have happy endings
So I can go to sleep.
'Til I awake in the morn
With lessons I can keep.

About the Author

Gordon Bostic was born in West Virginia and grew up in Virginia. A graduate of James Madison University and Fairleigh Dickinson University, he worked as a computer scientist and a software engineer for most of his life. He began writing at a young age as a way of expressing himself, his feelings, and his view of the world. Gordon has also had an interest in telling his stories in one way or another. *Bedtime Stories: A Child's Collection of Poems* is his second book of poetry. Gordon currently lives on the Jersey Shore with his wife, Susan.